LAST POEMS

OF

ELINOR WYLIE

LAST POEMS

OF

ELINOR WYLIE

POEMS TRANSCRIBED BY
JANE D. WISE
WITH OTHER POEMS HITHERTO UNPUBLISHED
IN BOOK FORM

FOREWORD BY
WILLIAM ROSE BENÉT

WITH A TRIBUTE TO ELINOR WYLIE BY
EDITH OLIVIER

"Into the hungry coffin and beyond it
A single uncorrupted drop of youth
Must live in elegy upon my lips
When I and chaos shall have come to grips."

DEDICATION

**Academy
Chicago**

Copyright© 1943 by Alfred A. Knopf
Copyright renewed 1970 by E.C. Rubenstein and Alfred A. Knopf

Academy Chicago edition 1982
All rights reserved
Academy Chicago
425 North Michigan Avenue
Chicago, Illinois 60611

Cover photograph: Elinor Wylie as a young woman. (Collection of Henry W. and Albert A. Berg Collection, The New York Public Library, Astor, Lenox, and Tilden Foundations, and Mr. and Mrs. Sydney Schiffer).

Library of Congress Cataloging in Publication Data

Wylie, Elinor Hoyt, 1885-1928.
    Last poems of Elinor Wylie.

    Includes index.
    I. Wise, Jane D.   II. Title.
PS3545,Y45L3   1982   811'.5'2   79-16672
ISBN 0-89733-012-9
ISBN 0-89733-011-0 pbk.

FOREWORD

THE SENSE in which the word "Last" is used of these poems by Elinor Wylie, now first brought together, is as "last in a series" of books. Some of the inclusions are, of course, early work. The wisdom of publishing this book may be called in question by those who believe that nothing but an author's very best should, after his or her death, be given to the world. There existed, however, the consideration that in various magazines and books certain poems remained which, it seemed to me, should be gathered together before, in the course of time, they were collected in some less appropriate fashion. I have purposely excluded lighter work of an entirely fugitive character, printing only such lighter verses as, from their epigrammatic nature and precise phraseology, seemed to enter the general domain of poetry. A few early objective poems, some in a direct dramatic style now temporarily out of fashion, still seem to me firm in structure and original in concept, and I make no apology for including them along with later and subtler work. Also I see no reason against combining the grave with the more frivolous. The poet's nature possessed both aspects.

There were among Elinor's papers certain characteristic pencilled and typed manuscripts. The deciphering and transcribing of the former was a task that might have balked even the poet herself, but it was undertaken by Jane D. Wise. Her success has been remarkable. Through her efforts, several lyrics, sonnets, and longer poems have been recovered that it would have been grievous to lose. Certain typed mss. have also been deemed characteristic enough to include here. Mr. Knopf has been sympathetic and helpful in causing to be reproduced certain of the holographs that will be of interest to students. Miss Wise had the reproductions made from enlarged microfilm.

When Elinor Wylie's "Collected Poems" were published I referred to a long poem, "The Golden Heifer," in the metre of her famous "Peregrine." More of this poem has now been recovered, and inasmuch as, though otherwise jaunty and even jocose, it possesses indubitable magic, perhaps it does not matter that it remains apparently unfinished. In a sense it does reach a proper conclusion; for the children with the miraculous animal, to which Elinor even refers as a "faun" (thus disallowing the deity of fields and herds an assumption of human shape), are led eventually to the Earthly Paradise of "Holy Brandan." That a pagan deity inhabiting an animal should eventually lead children, rendered wholly innocent, into a Celtic and hence Christian paradise, is not at all astonishing in a poem by Elinor Wylie. Elinor never through her life forgot the companionship of a particularly loved brother and sister, nor the imaginary adventures they had as children. I believe it was a dream of reunion with this sister and this brother that animated the ending of this poem, when the offspring of the imagined farmer undergo transfiguration as they quicken their pace toward a magical destination.

It is not claimed that there is anything here that surpasses Elinor's former work. But for the student of her work there are some interesting things. There is variety,

Elinor Wylie's study at 36 West 9th Street, New York City.
Photograph by the late Morrison Marsh.

too. For example, nothing could be more sophisticated than the first of the "Subversive Sonnets," nothing more disillusioned than the second, and yet the third attains an almost Shakespearian expression of wisdom. Again, one may ponder the exquisite simplicity of "With a Blue Honey-Jar," and contrast it with the bitterly realistic "From the Wall." There is simple and innocent beauty here, and playfulness, and wrath and irony. The nature of the poet defied the world's passion for pigeonholes.

A word on several poems: although "Les Lauriers Sont Coupés" appeared originally in Elinor's first little book, "Incidental Numbers," long since out of print, I include it here because it also exists in the "Contemporary Verse Anthology." In the back of her book, "Elinor Wylie: The Portrait of an Unknown Lady," Elinor's sister, Nancy Hoyt, included seven poems from "Incidental Numbers" — one, "The Knight Fallen On Evil Days" being very fine indeed — and "Sea-Blue Eyes" which was written at Somesville, Maine, in 1919 and published in *The Century Magazine*. I refer you to Nancy's book for those. But there is another sonnet, of about the time of her initial book, which Elinor once let me use in my *Saturday Review* column. It is the one "Written on the Flyleaf of John Webster's Plays." It was from Webster, it will be recalled, that Elinor eventually took the title of her first public book of poems, "Nets To Catch the Wind." Notes will be found at the end of this volume concerning all the poems included.

After Elinor's death — on January 2, 1929, to be exact — the distinguished English novelist, Edith Olivier, sent me the tribute which follows. She wrote me then:

I have felt impelled to write something about Elinor, and now I send you what I have written, as you may like to read it yourself or may think it might appear somewhere. She told me in that letter I had on Christmas Day — written I think on the last day of her life — that she had just finished arranging her poems for the Press, and I wondered if you would think that what I send you might appear as a little Prelude for that Volume. But in any case I give it to you to use as you like, and if you do use it anywhere, please alter and edit as you wish . . . I have written of her as I knew her, trying to convey something of the rarity of her nature.

At the time it was not possible to use Miss Olivier's gracious gift. When she sees it now, I hope it may remind her of the genuine and deep affection the poet had for her. To Elinor, Edith Olivier represented those noble and gallant qualities that adorn the England whose cause today is so utterly our own. To conclude; in a grim crisis, when we are left no choice but to fight destruction with destruction, I can only hope that these reliques, gay and tragic, of a great gift, may serve to remind the general public of abiding beauty.

WILLIAM ROSE BENÉT

New York City,
  June 27, 1942.

CONCERNING ELINOR WYLIE

I RECALL the first time that I saw Elinor Wylie. I had driven over, one Summer evening in England, to dine at a country house near by, and I stood for a few minutes in the hall, looking out upon a serene garden, from whence there came in, through the open door, a green reflected light, the songs of birds, and the scents of many flowers. The upper part of the staircase beside me was in shadow, but I heard a movement, and turned, to see Elinor coming down. I didn't know who she was. How finely she held herself, making a picture which remains in the mind, vivid and uneclipsed throughout the memories of our later friendship. She was wearing a dress made of stiff shiny silk, and it looked like frozen green water. She was tall, but at that moment, seen from below, she appeared more than usually so. She came holding herself very erect, with a smooth evenness of carriage, like those eastern women, who are accustomed to carry a pitcher of water on their heads. Her face was heart-shaped, and very white, and the copper-coloured hair curved nobly away from the sides of her forehead. Under the finely drawn eyebrows, " her eyes were agate," like those of the Miranda of one of her most characteristic poems; and the hand which rested on the banister was white, like a hand seen under water. I ought to have known at once that this was the writer of " The

Venetian Glass Nephew": instead, I wondered who she could be.

My memories of Elinor thus begin, very markedly, with the memory of her appearance, which always seemed to me, most essentially, the outer semblance of her spirit. It was beautiful, that appearance of hers, and consciously so. She loved beauty; sought it; created it; — in her person and her surroundings, as well as in her writing. It was, in a sense, the passion of her life. Hers was, throughout, the deliberate pursuit of a loveliness which she valued most, perhaps, when to others it might appear far-fetched and precious.

She seemed born to find the rare thing, to see it from an oblique angle, at some quick, coloured moment, and then to paint it in words of a daring subtlety. It was this which made her character, like her work, so individual. She did not write about "roses drenched with dew," but of the "*seedlings of another planet*": not about the lives and loves of those people (so dear to the Lending Library subscriber) "whom one would be glad to have in one's own drawingroom"; but of some

> *lightning-feathered falcon, leaping*
> *To trace a hieroglyph in heaven.*

One could not always follow her on foot: wings were needed.

Her phrases are packed with allusions. Few people realised the extent of Elinor's learning. Her novels were often looked upon as mere flights of fancy, — airy impossibilities floating in the clouds; while, instead, her fantastic creations were flowers with roots reaching down into unguessed deeps of erudition. "The Venetian Glass Nephew," for instance, absurd toy as he sounds, comes to life in the atmosphere of Renaissance Italy. " Mortal Image "* tells of something which never happened to Shelley, but the book compels belief by the truth of its picture of life a hundred years ago, and by its yard-by-yard knowledge of the southern states from the Atlantic to the Pacific in the year eighteen hundred and twenty-two. And how amusing, in " Mr Hodge and Mr Hazard " are the little touches which call up the talk of a by-gone day, — the books of the moment, the newspapers, the gossip, all meticulously correct.

Certainly Elinor Wylie was incurably scholarly, and throughout her life, she was as much student as poet. She read widely for all her novels, each one of which exists as the natural offspring of a mind saturated with the period described.

Her poems had the same character. They were full of the fruits of her reading. But her way of writing was so concise, that she could almost pack into one glittering line, the contents of some great dusty volume which she had found forgotten on the upper shelf in a country house library. No wonder it was sometimes hard to keep pace with her.

> The little sum of my experience
> Remains the sole contrivance I produce
> To weave this mesh, To colour and confuse
> These ragged syllables with soul and sense.

The lines come from one of the Sonnets in the group called " A Red Carpet for Shelley," and it is true that Elinor's poetry, like most poetry, for those who know its secret, was intensely personal. But her personality was a complicated one, and any picture of it must needs be baffling.

* The American title of this novel is " The Orphan Angel." — *Ed.*

Poetically Elinor had two masters. The first was Shelley.

Somewhere she has told us how she spent an evening once with Mr Roger Ingpen, " smiling with him at a hundred beloved recollections of someone we have never seen," and then they two compared their earliest memories of Shelley. The English poet was the companion of Elinor's soul. She knew nearly all Shelley's poems by heart, and could always finish any line quoted. His intimates were hers: every piece of his recorded conversation was familiar to her: his letters might all have been written to her. It was in some ways an even closer intimacy than is possible with a living person, for there the stream of life goes by, taking with it one thing after another to be forgotten in the past. The whole of Shelley's life lay recorded before Elinor. She was soaked in it, and it was with her always in the present. He was her life's strongest influence, — emotional, — intellectual, — artistic.*

Later on, Elinor read a great deal of Donne. Her poems shew his influence, but I think their two minds were naturally akin. She revelled, as he did, in " the Festivals and Pentecosts of Metaphysics." She liked Donne's packed style, his curious metaphors, his bold paradoxes. Throughout her last summer in England, Elinor carried everywhere with her the complete poetical works of Donne, and she read them again and again. The subjects he chose were subjects which she too would have chosen, and her treatment of a theme was often oddly like his. Neither she, nor this master of hers is " popular." The flavour of each of them is for the epicure's palate alone.

Sensitive as an artist, Elinor was equally sensitive as a woman. It was easy to wound her, but not easy to tell

* Note the tangential reference to Shelley in the octave of the last sonnet of the first section of the present collection. — *Ed.*

where she had been wounded, for she held her head up, and hid the poisoned arrow in her heart. But a chance word could make her deeply unhappy, and very often did. This quick sensitiveness of hers was sometimes rather amusingly shewn in her patriotic attitude. Elinor was an ardent patriot, being equally proud of her American citizenship and of her English descent. One of her great desires was to foster a sympathy and unity between the two nations to both of which she rejoiced to belong. She was quick to hear the least slur cast on one of her native lands by a citizen of the other, and she was always most American among the English, and most English among the Americans. She would rise with spirit to defend her absent country from attack, and could not easily forgive the attacker, however thoughtless and trivial his words.

To defend the absent or the criticised was natural to her, for Elinor was one of the most courageous of women. How great her physical courage was, no one knew who did not see her in those weeks of acute physical suffering which followed the accident in which she fractured her backbone. Confined to her bed, in one rigid and uncomfortable position, enduring continuous and intense pain, she talked brilliantly with her visitors, and when left alone she read all the books she could find on the subject of the French prisoners in England during the Napoleonic Wars. She had a fellow-feeling with them, she said, as she too was a prisoner, and she had it in her mind to write a romance of this period. This was one of the projects left unfinished at her death, as was also a little story which she had actually begun, the scene of which was laid in an imaginary New Forest village called *Autrelieu,* but pronounced *Atterley.* That name was most characteristic, — the sense of mellow distance which haunts the word " Autrelieu," and then the sharp tang in " Atterley," like a sudden box on the ears. Elinor liked such contrasts.

Doomed to die so soon and so suddenly, Elinor had all her life been companioned by the thought of death. Perhaps it had remained with her from that day in the library of the Washington house, when she " wondered why the bright creature should have died and fallen into dust." Through many of her poems there runs a poignant awareness of the ironic linking of an immortal spirit with a mortal frame.

> The small soul's dissolving ghost
> Must leave a heart-shape in the dust
> Before it is inspired and lost
> In God: I hope it must.

Sometimes she seemed almost too painfully preoccupied by memories of dissolution and decay, by the thought that

> The flying bone, the sighing breast
> One with nothingness is made;

and yet she had no fear of death. Rather she looked forward to it, much as she loved this earth. One of the poems written in the last months of her life was the " Little Prayer " which begins, " My best content were death "; and, reading this, no one who loved her can regret, for her, the swift and simultaneous ending of her youth, her beauty and her brilliancy.

For myself, her own words voice my feelings:

> I shall not sprinkle with dust
> A creature so clearly lunar;
> You must die — but of course you must —
> And better later than sooner.

. . . .

You will die, I suppose, before long.
Oh, worser sooner than later!

EDITH OLIVIER

The Daye House,
Quidhampton,
Salisbury,
England.

CONTENTS

☼

IV. POEMS FROM PERIODICALS, ETC.

Transcriber's Acknowledgment: *It gives me pleasure to thank Flora Belle Ludington, librarian of Mount Holyoke College; Tay Hohoff; Katherine Hayes and, especially, Eleanor Dayton for their help to me.*

J. D. W.

I. NEW POEMS AND SONNETS

TRANSCRIBED FROM HOLOGRAPH MSS.

BY JANE D. WISE

Under oak, ash and thorn . . .

BELTANE

Under oak, ash and thorn
My soul was born.
Under thorn, oak and ash
My body bent to the lash.
Under ash, thorn and oak
My heart broke.
Under oak, ash and thorn all three
I was nailed to a tree.

"SINCE WE CAN NEITHER
RUN NOR HIDE—"

Since we can neither run nor hide
Stand still, myself, and take the missile
Upon the sinister left side
And welcome it, and let it nestle
Against you so, and smooth its ruffled
Plumes, and stroke their down in peace.
And thus shall the pursuit be baffled
And we survive a breathing space.
Since we by no means may escape
By climbing up, by crouching lower
Let us assume a different shape
To meet the sharp and pointed shower,
This blast that penetrates and threatens
Now its arrows fly in sheaves.
Stand tranquil as a tree that sweetens
The winds that violate its leaves.

I saw Milton stand alone . . .

I saw Milton stand alone
Save for great Lord Verulam,
Bearing the philosopher's stone.
And the Pentecostal lamb
Was at Milton's side, his fleece
Bright as Jason's out of Greece.

Against them came a host
Shelley stricken to the heart
White like St. Sebastian's ghost
And taking still the weaker part
For her who quenched his keenest fires.
And flung him headlong from her spires.

GREEN APPLE

In England's green and pleasant land
I plucked an apple greener still;
I took the apple in my hand
As women will.

I bit the apple through and through.
The juice was sharp and clean and cold;
It tasted of a nectar new
Sprung from an old.

Its juice was bitter to taste as brine,
But sweet to smell as honey-breath;
It seemed a thin, precarious wine
Wrung out from death.

It smelt of lilacs and of salt,
Of juniper and balsam trees;
Though it was bitter to a fault
It breathed of these.

Unto its taste my palate clove;
I loved its flavour sharp as thorn.
This nuttiness I had known to love
Since I was born.

Some love the saps of west and south
And some the apple sharp and cold
And may it come to as fair a growth
As those who planted it foretold.

FIRTH OF FORTH

When I was living by the Firth of Forth
A lad of maybe nine or ten,
There rode a woman out of the north
As brave as twenty men.

Some said she came from Aberdeen,
Some, from a keep above Loch Lomond;
Some said she was a Tartar Queen
And some, the Scarlet Woman.

O she was fair, or fair enough,
Her body was straight as a new-cut lance;
Her heart was armoured by the stuff
That's iron to mischance.

Her hair fell to her tunic's hem
In colour like a fox's tail;
Her eyes had quicksilver in them,
Her freckled skin was pale.

And half the neighbours called her rich
And the other half declared her poor.
She built a house with a moated ditch
And a barricaded door.

My uncle, whose success in War
Had made him Justice of the Peace,
Felt her like salt and vinegar
In wounds that cried for grease. —

He chafed because she lived alone
And because she builded a gold-fish pool —
Because her doorstep was of stone
Her capuchin of wool.

And all that she could do was ill
And nothing she could do was right,
He'd seen her run on Warlock Hill
Hunting a wolf at night.

And if she was the King's cousin
Or gotten in the very pig's sty
He still convicted her of sin
Each time she met his eye.

She followed the hind, she flew ten hawks,
She fixed a cannon in her bower;
Her pennon on its silvered stalks
Wore fringes like a flower.

She builded a pavilion house
Upraised on gilded pairs of stilts;
In the clover field below her close
Her friends would ride at tilts.

She picked her friends like blackberries
Among the spikes of bramble hedges,
Or from the court, in twos and threes
Like jewelled stars and badges.

A table like a harvest moon,
The which had neither foot nor head,
Stood in her halls both night and noon
Most excellently spread.

Her wine was sweet as a yellow rose leaf
Her butter and cheese were never rancid;
Some got capon and some got beef,
But each got what he fancied.

Upon the Eve of Christmas Morn,
Being sick of crusts and stirabout,
I scrambled through the wall of thorn
And slid the frozen moat.

A grove of holly bushes stood
Drawn crescent-wise around the porches;
The snow was stained with dragon's blood
That dripped from twenty torches.

The snow was white as cygnet-down,
The dawn was pearl, the torches crimson,
The lady wore a velvet gown
Plum-coloured like a damson.

Upon the Eve of Christmas
                Were
Being nale of crust o
                this burnt
I scrambled through the wall
                of them
And shed the frozen moat.

A grove of holly bushes stood
Drawn crescent-wise around the porches
The snow was strewn...
That dripped from...
The snow was white as cygnet down
The dawn was pearl, that tender cream
The lady wore a velvet gown
Plum coloured like a damson...

Her hair was a sheaf of golden grain
Her lips were petals shaped for...

Upon the Eve of Christmas Morn, . . .

Eat and said, and ask for more
For this is one of your

saurine taverns

I saw my uncle at his
door

His eyes were limestone caverns

My blood ran cold, & fever-hot
~~He leaned upon his~~ crystals

I knew at once he was the devil
My grandfather was his land

My grandmere came from Seville Spain

" ~~Dear heart~~
Come in dear heart, the
lady ~~said~~ spoke
I heard her crazy words
& shivered
Her words were sharp as
a silver lancet
they ~~with~~ thinned of valves
note
And I fell down in sunult

" Eat," she said, " and ask for more . . .

Her hair was a sheaf of golden grain,
Her lips were petals shaped for courage.
She said, " Have you come for marzipane
Or have you come for porridge? "

She gave me fruit of the wild grapevine,
A comb of honey and an apple,
And I could swear she gave me wine
From out an ivory nipple.

And venison from a silver plate.
She cried the servants to their carving,
She laughed and wept the while I ate,
" Good God, the boy is starving! "

" Eat," she said, " and ask for more
For this is one of your sovrin's taverns."
I saw my uncle at the door
His eyes were brimstone caverns.

My blood ran cold, and fever-hot,
I knew at once he was the Devil;
My grandfather was a Hieland Scot,
My grandam came from Seville.

" Come in, dear heart," the lady spoke,
Her voice was sharp as a silver lancet;
My little thread of valour broke
And I fell down insensate.

THREE ELEGIES

Keats was a chymist
Who took the moon to wife;
She kissed him for a wedding gift
And took away his life.
The cruel moon diminished him —
O pitiless Phoebe —
Fanny Brawne finished him,
He died in Rome of T.B.

Byron was a nobleman
Who lived like a swine;
Half of him was common muck
And half of him divine.
To serve the God of Love he
Slaved like a coal-heaver.
He died at Missolonghi
Of malarial fever.

Shelley was a gentleman
Who spent himself like gold,
But all the love he had to give
Was silver bright and cold.
Heaven he could reach; he
Married Godwin's daughter.
He died near Lerici
Of breathing sea-water.

The chymist and the nobleman,
The young Sussex squire,
Scale no more the slopes of Time
With their souls of fire.
Yet we are not fireless
For all their dying;
We have the wireless
And commercial flying.

SUBVERSIVE SONNETS

I

Take now the burning question of morality:
I love to keep myself unto myself,
To lock the door with exquisite finality,
To place the sugar-loaf upon the shelf.
Is this a virtue? Surely it is vice's
Most pinched ungenerous shape, to so refuse
A lover marzipane and lemon ices
Because he may have mud upon his shoes?

I am not proud because I hide such comfits
And comforts in a private cabinet;
They might be fiery medicine for his dumb fits
Of grief, or wine to win him to forget.
Shall I as holy chastity profess
What is mere tidiness and old-maidishness?

II

If one would dare to act upon the maxim
Which poor experience twenty times hath proven,
He might shake off the spotted beast that hacks him
And at the last escape Prince Satan's oven.
For it is true and no man may refute it,
Save clever sophists whom the just disparage,
If you've a heart it's better to uproot it
Betray your love and ride in Mammon's carriage

Over the corpses of the kind and gentle;
Strike down the weak; misuse your proper puissance
And no one then will call you sentimental
And no one will consider you a nuisance.
Be foul, be false, defend no virtuous quarrel;
Your grateful friends will crown your name with
    laurel.

III

Only a fool will call a fool a knave.
The second seeks a temporal advantage
Whereas the first goes naked to his grave,
Fallen to impecunious and gaunt age.
An honest man who calls a knave a fool
Is honest then as any mortal dust is;
His policy proves it: but reverse the rule,
He is less honest by his word's injustice.

The poor unlucky fool who travels late
Is plucked by knaves of all his copper farthings,
But honest men with prayer appropriate
His broken crystals and his tarnished star-things.
Name me, fond slave, the master whom thou
    shunnest:
Is he a knave, or devilishly honest?

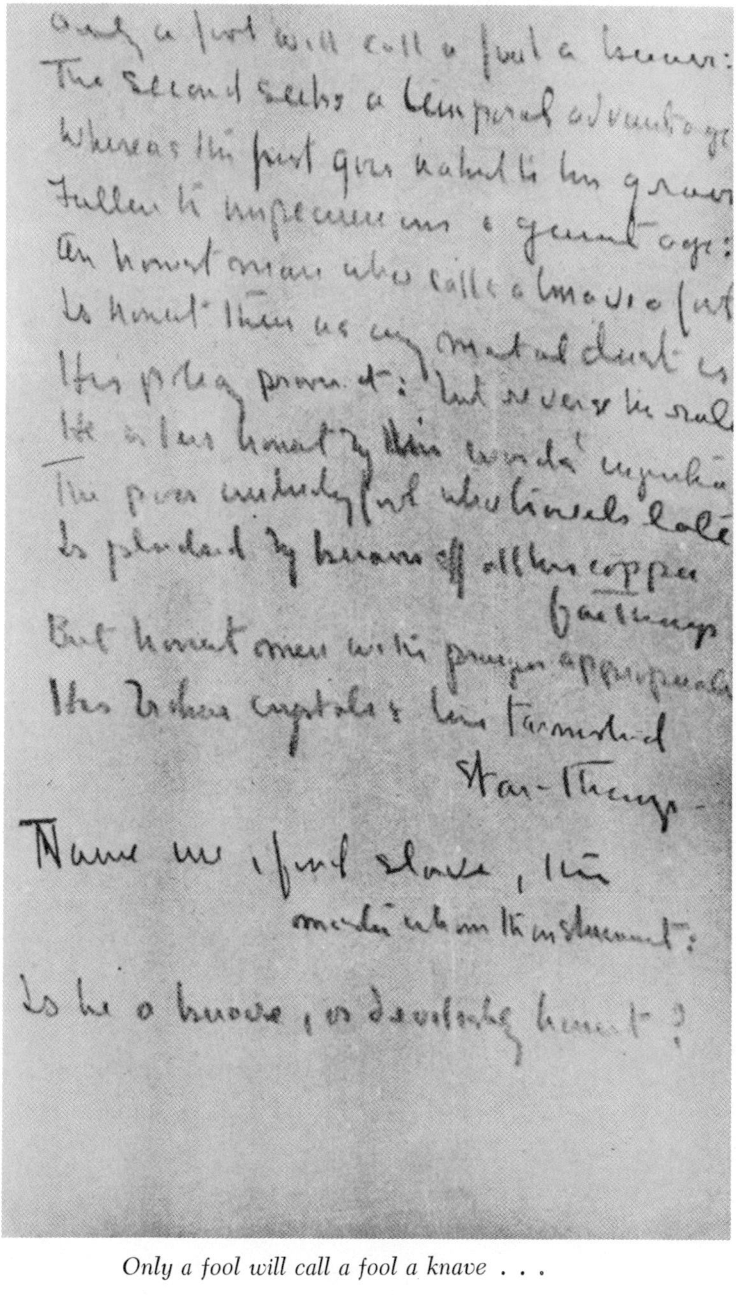

Only a fool will call a fool a knave:
The second seeks a temporal advantage
Whereas the fool goes naked to his grave
[illegible]
An honest man who calls a knave a fool
Is honest then as any mortal [illegible]
[illegible]
[illegible]
The poor unlucky fool who [illegible]
Is plundered by knaves of all his copper farthings
But honest men with proper [illegible]
[illegible]

[illegible]

Name me a fool slave, [illegible] instrument:

Is he a knave, or devilishly honest?

Only a fool will call a fool a knave . . .

SONNET

Courage and lovingkindness are approved
Superior virtues set above the rest
And I have long admitted they are blest
And followed them religiously, and loved;
But now the shadow of the sun has moved
To frighten me, and it is manifest
That yet another quality has dressed
Myself in steel, and helmetted and gloved.

This grace is dignity: sheer courage faints
And kindness calls the mimes and beggars in
And grins indecorous as any sin:
Then dignity is numbered with the saints,
Who locks my door on treachery and murder
And sweeps my hearth and sets my house in
  order.

SONNET

Is he not fortunate that he is freed
From the chill mortal burdens of my nature?
For he, a fiery and flying creature
Stooped ever to the level of my need
And it were monstrous and unfair indeed
If I were long permitted to disfeature
His grace; and lean against his greater stature
And shelter in his heart, and make it bleed.

And are you as unlucky to inherit
The loving obligation of a slave?
Your body still is bound upon your spirit
And I will serve it to the extreme grave
And wash the heavy grains of man's despair
From off its feet, and dry them with my hair.

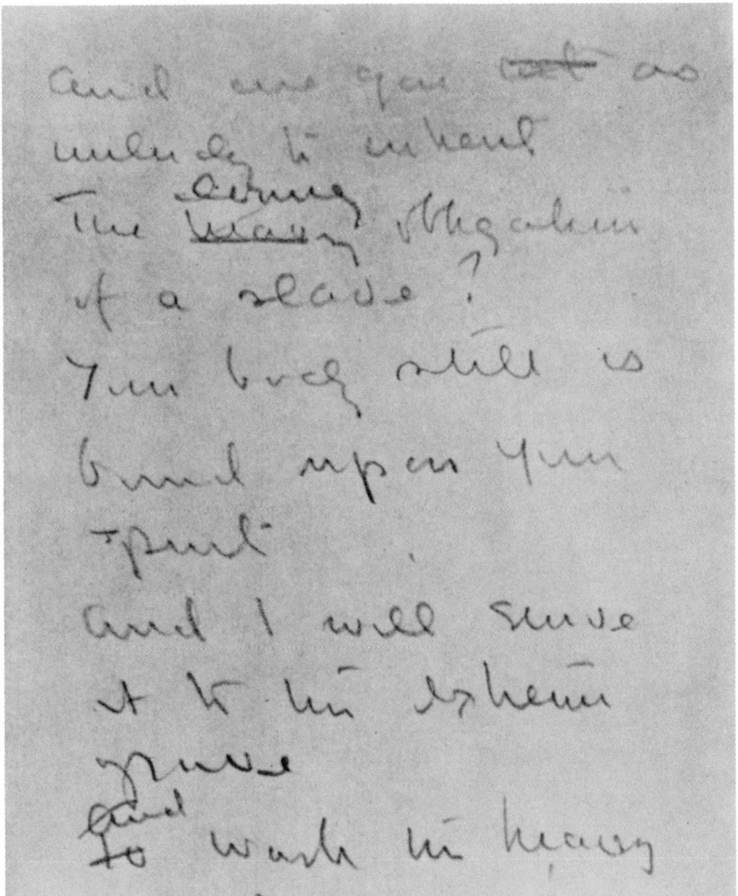
And are you ~~at~~ as
unlucky to inherit
The aching heavy obligation
of a slave?
Your body still is
bound upon your
spirit
And I will serve
it to the ashen
grave
~~To~~ And work in heavy
grains of man's
despair
Then: It ~~you~~ do fret,
& drag them with my
hair.

And are you as unlucky to inherit . . .

THE THREAD

Imagination makes a skein
Traversing distances in flight,
Drawn out to longer lines than rain
Falling from nothing in the night.

The hempen strand is twisted fear,
The silk is anger — broken thru —
The smooth is tinseled with a tear,
The rough is spangled with a hue.

But one most diligently sought
Is smaller than the clutch of sense
And this alone conveys a thought
Along its fine-spun permanence.

II. THE GOLDEN HEIFER

TRANSCRIBED FROM HOLOGRAPH MS.
BY JANE D. WISE

THE GOLDEN HEIFER

' At seven and twenty '
Thomas Dacre
Saved a plenty
And bought an acre,
Married his Sara,
Signed in the vestry,
Washed with Madeira
The wedding pastry.
He bought it freehold
And married her proper;
Having let the sea hold
His every copper
On several sagas
Southward, nor'ward;
Now rutabagas
Were his henceforward.

If he was crabbed
His wife had patience;
Wild as a rabbit
With his relations,
She'd smile in silence
When her own came over
From the Channel Islands.

They'd a bit in clover;
They called the Paddock.
He was glad he builded.
He'd drop his mattock
When silver-gilded
Stood the straggly orchard
Of pear and apple.

Though she took church hard
And he took chapel
They drew no moral.
He loved a sermon
And she a chorale.
Church was pure Norman,
Chapel, pine and varnish,
But her mother was Jersey
And his was Cornish.
So it seems a mercy
That both were Christians.

They summered and wintered
And asked no questions
Till their lives were splintered.
When his need was sorest
At forty-seven
She left the Forest
For the Courts of Heaven;
And he considered —
With the season rainy

And he thus widowed
With his daughter Jenny
And one boy shifty
And one boy sullen
And he near fifty
And the stalks of mullein
Crowding the sorrel
To kill the barley,
And the perry barrel
Stove in by Charley,
And Tom, the other,
With his queer, cold anger —
That the children's mother
Might have waited longer.
She'd crept cat-footed
Out of all this muddle
And left him rooted
In a barnyard puddle
Where his boots were squelching
And his hands sweat clammily
And hell yawned belching
For the whole damn family.

He took to drinking
With a sultry thirst born
Of twisted thinking.
John, the first-born,
Michael, the second,
Were nailed down firmly

In oak, he reckoned,
And covered warmly.
Hughie, the third one
Whom he'd whipped so often
Enjoyed the guerdon
Of a fine safe coffin.
So, in private,
And some confusion,
He'd arrive at
This conclusion —
By whiskey-toddy
Moved and carried
That everybody
Should be dead and buried.

The three survivors
Of all this worry
Were deep-sea divers
Where fish were furry;
Beneath thick foliage.
Where light was greenish
All their knowledge
Must begin and finish.
They went walking
With foxes and coneys;
Charles did the talking
While Tom changed ponies;
But Jen was queerest.
She caught green adders,

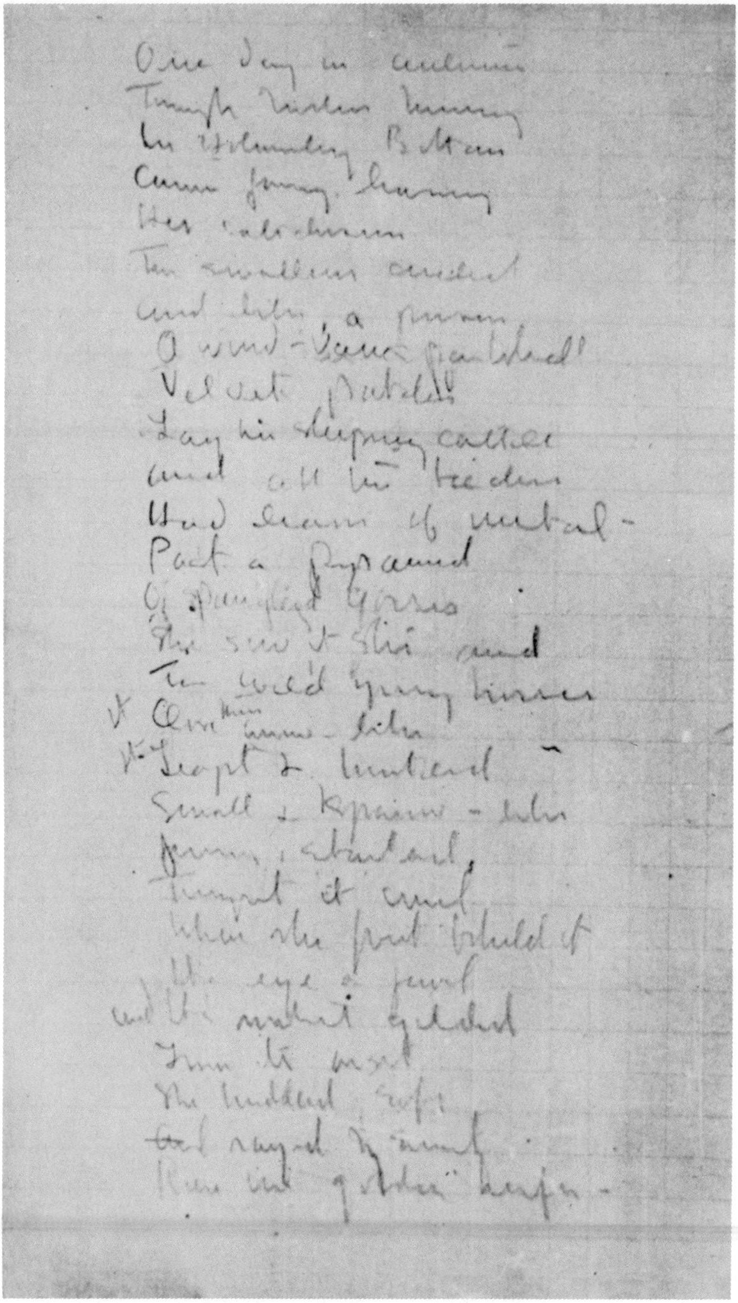

One day in Autumn . . .

And she saw clearest
The rainbow ladders
Erect in bracken,
Belaced with colour;
And she could reckon
To a Spanish dollar
The gold and silver
Which slept thereunder;
She was a delver
In fear and wonder.

One day in Autumn
Through bushes burning
In Holmsley Bottom
Came Jenny, learning
Her catechism.
The swallows circled
And like a prism
A wind-vane sparkled.
Velvet patches
Lay the sleeping cattle
And all the beeches
Had leaves of metal.
Past a pyramid
Of spangled gorses
She saw it stir amid
The wild young horses
It clove them, arrow-like,
It leapt and hurtled;

Small and sparrow-like
Jenny, startled,
Thought it cruel
When she first beheld it,
Its eye a jewel
And its nostril gilded.
From its onset
She huddled, safer;
Rayed by sunset
Ran the golden heifer.

Although the season
Was apple-scented,
The boys had reason
To be discontented.
They schemed and plotted
Over a plateful
Of cream, gold-clotted.
They were not ungrateful
For the jellied quinces'
Amber translucence.
They lived like princes
But they were a nuisance —
With all and sundry —
To Thomas their parent.
To leave the country
And turn knights-errant
They now decided,
To seek their fortunes,

Being largely guided
By older urchins.

They sold sweet cider
To the Queen's Head Tavern.
London the spider
In her smoky cavern
Was wreathed with Circe's
Rings and necklace;
Their father's curses
Had made them reckless.

Their fancies tramped on
To fire the river
Through Southampton
And Micheldiver;
Taking Surrey
Along the Hog's back
They would hurry,
To push the fogs back
From London Tower
And tall St. Paul dome.
Full of power
Free from thralldom,
They'd send up prayers
And sing them solemn
To be Lord Mayors.
By Nelson's column
They'd kneel in cinder

To ask the lions
To make them tinder
Giving defiance
In flame, to trouble.
Over their porridge
They blew this bubble
In the blood of courage.

As they sat in shadow
Counting gold in coppers,
The poor old widow
Who cooked their suppers
And darned their clothing —
Being but a woman —
Noticed nothing
In the least uncommon.
She saw no bannered
Knights in armour
But two bad-mannered
Sons of a farmer.

Under the moon, a
Girl rode straddle
Proud as Una
In her lion-saddle;
Without a stirrup
And without a bridle;
White as Europe
In the Pagan idyll;

Crossing the valley
Like a silver-laden
Slave-drawn galley;
Brave as a maiden
Whom Caracalla had
Killed by leopards;
Strong as Galahad;
Safe as the shepherd's
Yeanling lamblet;
Wild as the lady
Loved by Hamlet;
Like a mermaid steady
On a milk-white charger,
With a sea-green trident —
Their mouths grew larger,
Their brown eyes widened
When their father's daughter
Between rows of poplar
Ran like water
But swifter, suppler, —
Sliding colder,
Brighter, briefer,
Riding the shoulder
Of the golden heifer.

Thomas, the farmer,
Cross and sleepy
Came to his dormer.

The thing looked creepy,
It gave him gooseflesh
And he suffered torments.
When spirits loose flesh
They may take on garments
Starred and speckled
With phosphorescence.
His hair roots prickled
At a ghostly presence,
His half-clothed body
Shrunk with amazement,
His knuckles bloody
Where he'd broke the casement.
Green and sickened
He stood and trembled
As the creature quickened,
Slowed and ambled.
He made a gesture
At necromancies.
He screamed " You'll pasture
In Sara's pansies
No Doomsday pageant
Of god-damned gypsies! "
The man imagined
Apocalypses.

Down he clattered
With hanging braces.
The children scattered

Like pony races.
His loud " I'll catch you
And cure your knavery "
Met a statue
Gilt and ivory,
A shape that Pluto
Had unfettered,
Benvenuto
Could not have bettered
On sphynx or cherub
That smooth enamel,
Or ever Arab —
Spurring his camel
To snare a burnished
Mare from mirages
Having long furnished
Steeds for Pashas —
Lassoed a mate for
This magic creature,
Or Bishop paid for
A bowl or pitcher
With a dolphin handle
Or a swan-necked flagon
That could hold a candle
To her grace — nor dragon
Leaving his cold den
To drink sun-fever
Ever shone so golden
As the golden heifer.

A deer! Lord Lucas's,
Or strayed from Beaulieu!
Yellow as crocuses
He thought it truly,
Hardly duller
Than a new brass button
Ringed with colour.
If this beast were mutton
And fit for tallow,
And finding's keeping —
But a farmer or fellow — !

His children sleeping
Under their gable
Heard the clanging
Door of the stable
Which seemed a church in
The middle ages
Where a painted virgin
Received the Magis
With a crib over lit
By that light of Titian's
They pulled the coverlet
Over such visions.

When dawn was breaking
They rose up gently
Scarcely speaking
Yet feeling saintly

34

And strangely armoured
Against all peril.
Dawn, in the farm yard,
Was bright as beryl *
And they the Magis.
Through the isthmus
By easy stages,
Over the deserts
Vast and arid,
Past all hazards
They had carried
Love like a censer.
Now the puzzle
Had an answer.
They touched the muzzle,
And it felt silkier
Than a damask petal.
Jen was a Melchior,
Stout and little;
But the boys were rougher
By human nature
With love to offer
To the velvet creature.
Over and over
They kissed her and meant it.
The faun ate clover
And seemed contented.

* Note: The next line in the original has been erased. The rhyme was
" Christmas." — Ed.

Before the rooster
Wakened Thomas
They had loosed her.
" Take you from us
That he daren't! "
They felt the heresy
Of their parent
As conspiracy
Of happy rebels
Marching to battle
In holy fables.
They left the cattle,
They left the poultry,
They stepped out proper.
The day was sultry,
The sun was a copper
Rose, and spherical,
But the clouds were pearly.
It seemed a miracle
Had come to Burley.
An amethyst church
With a tower of shadows
Hung over Christchurch
And its water meadows,
And the western
Way lay farther
Opening a postern
To the Courts of Arthur.

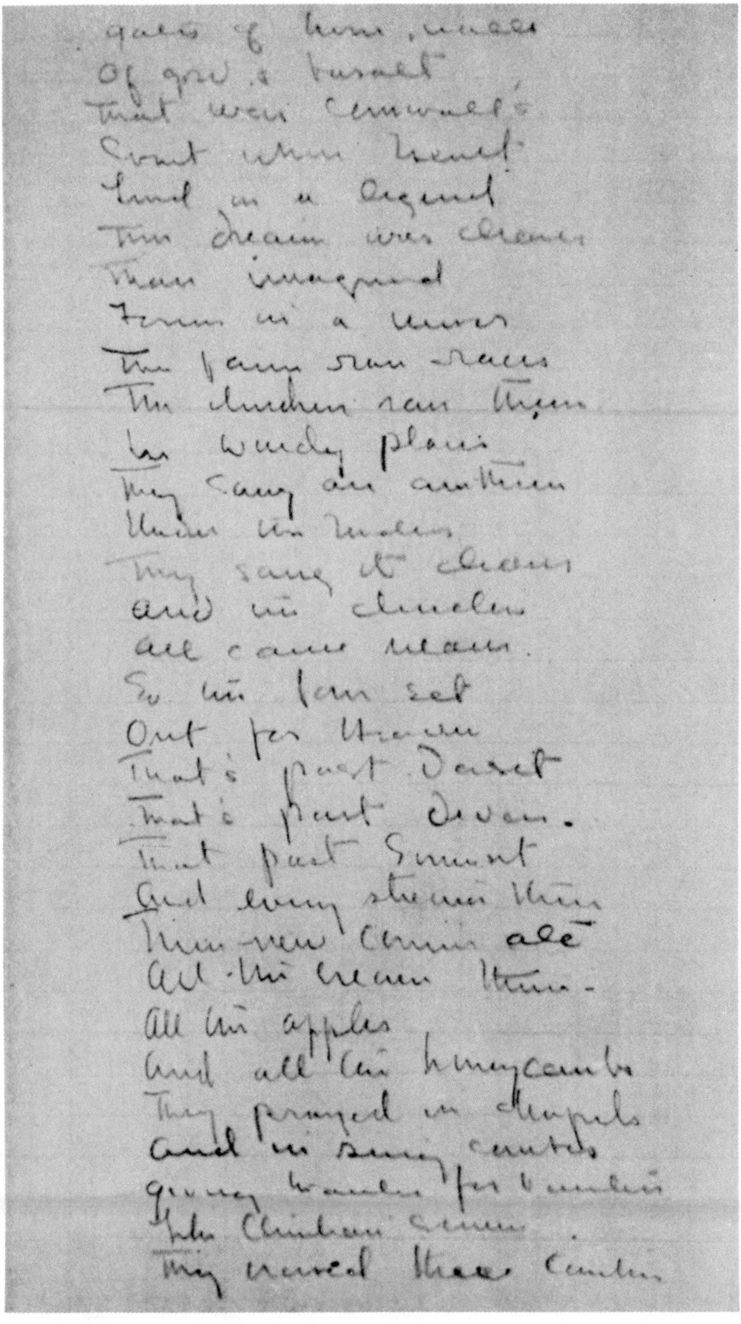

Gates of horn, walls . . .

Gates of horn, walls
Of gold and basalt:
That was Cornwall's
Coast where Iseult
Lived in a legend.
Their dream was clearer
Than imagined
Forms in a mirror.
The faun ran races
The children ran them.
In windy places
They sang an anthem
Under the birches.
They sang it clearer,
And the churches
All came nearer.
So the four set
Out for Heaven
That's past Dorset,
That's past Devon,
That's past Somerset
And every stream there;
These newcomers ate
All the cream there,
All the apples
And all the honey combs.
They prayed in chapels
And in sunny coombes,

Giving thanks for bounties
Like Christian sinners.
They crossed three counties
Before their dinners —
Jam, and chicken
Which Jenny roasted
High among bracken
Silver-frosted
By ocean bubbles.
They were hungry
And they had no troubles.
No one angry
Impugned their morals.
They went swimming
In a pool of corals.
The faun lay dreaming.

They flew onward
As the sun was falling,
They flew sunward
Through sea gulls calling;
The stars were bobbing
Like grain in a hopper,
The boys were sobbing,
" I want my supper! "
Jenny was silent.
She had to love them.
They saw an island
Rise above them.

The boys were ravening —
It was sweet to land on
A quiet evening
In holy Brandon.

III. OTHER POEMS NOW FIRST PRINTED

ROSES IN WINTER

This is the city where the spring
Blooms in the sky before its hour
In sunsets fleeter than a wing
And sweeter than a flower.

Beyond this steely net of trees
Clouds blossom soft and tropical,
As down chill iron trellises
The tenderest petals fall.

Here on this pavement, glazed with ice,
Lie mirrored in the stony shine
Exotic colors, warm as spice,
And glamorous as wine.

The cruel cold shall freeze our blood
For many a night, for many a day;
These rich skies hold each rose in bud
We pluck, full-blown, in May.

CITY MORNING

The river whistles
Grow up like thistles,
The bells are thorns to
Split the morning,
But country murmurs
That waken farmers
Are soft as wool where
Lambs are borning.

The El's long rattle
Has spikes of metal,
The traffic sweeps with
An iron besom,
But somewhere, seemly,
The trees stir dimly
And one cockcrow is
A yellow blossom.

SPRING

Madness flies in the spring,
In moonlight running to waste,
Something brushes my lips like a sting
With a piercing taste,

Burning my face like a lash;
Whole cedar-forests of ships
Foundered; cities fallen to ash;
Their blood on my lips;

Bright atoms of air, that must
Forever tremble and shine.
I am less than nothing to their blowing dust:
They are nothing to mine.

FROM THE WALL

Woman, be steel against loving, enfold and defend you,
Turn from the innocent look and the arrogant tongue;
You shall be coppery dross to the purses that spend you;
Lock up your years like a necklace of emeralds strung.

Lock up your heart like a jewel; be cruel and clever;
Woman, be strong against loving, be iron, be stone;
Never and never and never and never and never
Give for the tears of a lover a tear of your own.

Cover the clutch of your greed with a velvety gloving;
Take from the good if you can, from the vile if you must;
Take from the proud and alone, from the cowardly
    loving;
Hold out your hands for the pity; accept of the lust.

AT THE HOSPITAL

I wandered in a draughty corridor
Which smelled of death, and saw this hateful
      thing.
A comely youth had motored there to bring
Some lady charity, whom he waited for;
To him now turned, in tragic comradeship
A little man, untidy, spent, and grey
With " This is anxious work, this waiting, eh? "
The sleek one stared,with silent, scornful lip.

I have seen cruelty grinning like a skull
Or knitted in a murderer's grimace
But never warped to so obscene a face
As that, unmoved, contemptuous, cold and dull.
Desperate, I smiled, and clutched the shabby
      coat,
My fingers itching for the other's throat.

WITH A BLUE HONEY–JAR
FULL OF FLOWERS

Here, within this honey-jar,
Rose and honeysuckle are;
Keep it so, a turquoise shell
Of sweetness like a honey-cell;
Keep it so it may not miss
The richer brew, being filled with this,
Fresher and more exquisite
Than wine the bees distil from it

A SKYLARK AT STEEPLETOP

Upon the levels of the air
You live; nor now belong
Where once ungrateful valleys were
Content to prove you wrong.

And now 'tis depths, not distances,
By which you measure space:
The skies are your peculiar seas;
The moon your special grace.

It makes an island more exempt
From pestilence and wars
Than any you had ever dreamt
Might lie between the stars.

Yet this for you, who never stop,
Grows narrow in the night,
And here and there a mountain-top
May penetrate your flight.

And here your honest lover seeks
A solitude of joys
And all devoted mountain peaks
Play echo to your voice.

And one of these, which sets a sail
Of snow against the wind,
Has caught a golden nightingale
Will whistle to your mind.

Elude the one, and lose the two,
And choose the lucky third,
And listen, while the leaves are new,
To that enchanting bird.

I'll spread my darker plumes and come,
And on the evening hill,
Entreat her magic to be dumb
And bid myself be still.

And music shall forbear to sing,
And silence shall be proud
Because of some secretive thing
Which cries within a cloud.

In vales of Rother and of Thames
Shall sorrow grow rotten-ripe,
But the loving hills shall leap like lambs
That hear the shepherd's pipe.

And you, impulsive to forgive
Valleys of weeping rain,
Shall leave the level air, and live
On English earth again.

So like a skylark you shall drop
Into the water meadows:
The nightingales of Steepletop
Must mourn forever widows.

FAR AWAY

Now stars burn out to ashes
and lawns are spread with lace
and morning lifts her lashes
to look upon your face.

Now trees are silver tasselled
and clouds are water-spun
and I rise up undazzled
Who only see the sun.

SILVER BELLS AND COCKLE SHELLS

Once I fled as children flee
Far from my desire;
Then my freedom was to me
As Promethean fire.

I fell in with something dark;
Something like a man;
Then I took my Titan-spark,
Turned about and ran.

Drinking fire's delicious dew,
Dancing like a star,
On I flew, on I flew,
Far and very far.

I fell in with someone kind,
And he gave me gloves,
Lovely cloaks with ermine lined,
Several kind of loves.

In his arms I learned to sleep,
From his hand I fed,
Till I left my friend to weep;
Far away I fled.

Tasting air's enchanting speed
Far I fled away,
Till I found a bitter need
On a rainy day.

I fell in with someone good
Standing in the rain,
Gave me kisses, gave me food
Sweet as manna-grain.

In his arms I learned to rest;
Took his sugar-bread,
Till I left my lover's breast;
Far away I fled.

Do I flee, loving flight?
Do I flee to find
Something lost, something light,
Something half-unkind?

WITCHES

Green eyes, gold hair, great beauty,
Have witches while they're girls,
Or dark eyes soft and sooty,
Bright lips and cloudy curls.

Though this one looks like Helen,
And that one looks like Eve,
They'll slice your heart like a melon
With never a by-your-leave.

So mind your mother and daddy
And do as you are told,
Or the witches will gobble you up, my lad,
When they are starved and old.

"—IN A COUNTRY CHURCHYARD"

The vast majority of my friends have stated
That, at the long irrevocable last,
They hope that their remains may be cremated
And then discreetly scattered on the blast.

The more romantic souls, whose dreams are
    vaguer,
Rejecting still the dull subterrene grave,
Entreat, like Mr. Swinburne's Meleager,
To be committed to the cooling wave.

Since buried bones eventually grow rotten
And mortuary art offends good taste
They one and all demand to be forgotten
Completely, and in quite indecent haste.

The weaker spirits may perhaps desire
A small receptacle or sculptured urn;
Others would have us pour upon the pyre
Spices and salt and purple wine to burn.

And some indulge a dim Egyptian vision
Of pyramids and bitumen and myrrh.
I disagree: I know with great precision
The ultimate decorum I prefer.

Give me a linen shroud, an oaken coffin
 Unpiercable, though silver trumpets called,
Chisel my name in stone which time may soften
While trees are dark and turf is emerald.

But carve that word — because I'm sentimental —
In sandstone which shall yield it to the rain
Before the years, with fingers slow and gentle,
Have smoothed it out forever from your brain.

"ADVICE TO THE LOVELORN"

Lest intellect should be submerged
When you have ceased to starve your passion,
Condemn your body to be scourged
By fasting in another fashion.

Imagination leaps from this,
Still spirited, but wilder, thinner;
So, if you hunger for a kiss,
Take it, but go without your dinner.

CHINESE PRIEST

"Man cannot live by bread alone?" What man?
There speaks in pride the haughty Aryan,
Demanding spiritual plums and spice
While the meek Orient subsists on rice.

SONNET

Whether you grind your teeth in giving it
As blood to quench inordinate demands,
Or grant it with fastidious white hands
To medicine a beggar's dreaming-fit,
Or toss it like an apple, or permit
A silver trickle to the tortured sands,
Or warm a cry in golden swaddling-bands,
Its sevenfold virtues lie securely knit.

O, cast it like a stone, or let it rain
Singing all wounds to sleep with balsam petals;
Send it to Babylon, call it home again;
Into whatever strangeness it is bent
You cannot change the strangeness of its
    metals
Or make them other than beneficent.

SONNET

When, in the dear beginning of the fever
Whose one remedial physic must be death,
I drew the light and unembittered breath
Of ecstasy, then was I brave and clever;
No pinch of dust presumed to whisper " never ";
The soul had exorcised the body's wraith,
In sacred madness and severer faith,
And this delirium should endure forever.

Then was my throat obedient as a reed
Wherein a demigod is audible;
But now its stops are practised to foretell
Only the mortal doom, the murderous deed:
Yet, if my love is pleased to whistle once,
The silver still cries out above the bronze.

A LODGING FOR THE NIGHT

If I had lightly given at the first
The lightest favours that you first demanded;
Had I been prodigal and open-handed
Of this dead body in its dream immersed;
My flesh and not my spirit had been pierced:
Your appetite was casual and candid;
Thus, for an hour, had endured and ended
My love, in violation and reversed.

Alas, because I would not draw the bolt
And take you to my bed, you now assume
The likeness of an angel in revolt
Turned from a low inhospitable room,
Until your fiery image has enchanted
And ravished the poor soul you never wanted.

THE PILLARS OF THE TEMPLE

The eye of the beholder being put out
What else remains to make us beautiful?
The legendary pattern of a skull
Lapped casually in a linen clout
Coloured by death; this only the devout
And noble vision serves: obscene and dull
Save when some transmutation shall annul
The soft decaying clay, the bones of doubt.

This love is not a curled equivocal Eros
Blind from his birth: he has been cruelly blinded:
The invincible sinews of his heart are strung
Above revenge: such were the elder heroes.
He could put forth his strength, were he so minded,
And grind us into particles of dung.

IV. POEMS FROM PERIODICALS, ETC.

"LES LAURIERS SONT COUPÉS"

Ah, love, within the shadow of the wood
The laurels are cut down; some other brows
May bear the classic wreath which Fame allows
And find the burden honorable and good.
Have we not passed the laurels as they stood —
Soft in the veil with which the Spring endows
The wintry glitter of their woven boughs —
Nor stopped to break the branches while we could?

Ah, love, for other brows they are cut down.
Thornless and scentless are their stems and flowers,
And cold as death their twisted coronal.
Sweeter to us the sharpness of this crown;
Sweeter the wildest roses which are ours;
Sweeter the petals, even when they fall.

WRITTEN ON THE FLYLEAF OF
JOHN WEBSTER'S PLAYS

Having so long walked hand in hand with Hell
I find these gentry little less than kin;
I speak their sulphurous language; we begin
Straightway to cap each other's jests, and tell
Fantastical adventures which befell
At midnight, some eccentric court within —
Where fiery anger plotted with pale sin —
Crime's sanctuary, murder's citadel.

Fouler the cruelties which desecrate
These later days, to poison heart and mind,
And strangle, with the bloody hand of Hate,
The thrice-stabbed soul; from such I turn to find
The black Calabrian comrade in my fate,
And Corombona, as a sister, kind.

SOUTH OF THE POTOMAC

Wild honey in the honey-comb,
And swarms of golden bees,
These are as sumptuous as Rome,
Rich as the Chersonese.

Not Tamburlaine's Persepolis
Nor vaulted Ctesiphon·
Were jewelled as this serpent is
Which stretches in the sun.

And this red earth beneath my hand,
Which burns my hand like fire,
Is barbarous as Samarcand,
Imperial as Tyre.

THE CHILD ON THE CURBSTONE

The headlights raced; the moon, death-faced,
Stared down on that golden river.
I saw through the smoke the scarlet cloak
Of a boy who could not shiver.

His father's hand forced him to stand,
The traffic thundered slaughter;
One foot he thrust in the whirling dust
As it were running water.

As in a dream I saw the stream
Scatter in drops that glistened;
They flamed, they flashed, his brow they
    splashed,
And danger's son was christened.

The portent passed; his fate was cast,
Sea-farer, desert-ranger.
Tearless I smiled on that fearless child
Dipping his foot in Danger.

THE LOST PATH

The garden's full of scented wallflowers,
And, save that these stir faintly, nothing stirs;
Only a distant bell in hollow chime
Cried out just now for far-forgotten time,
And three reverberate words the great bell spoke.
The knocker's made of brass, the door of oak,
And such a clamor must be loosed on air
By the knocker's blow that knock I do not dare.
The silence is a spell, and if it break,
What things, that now lie sleeping, will awake?

Are simple creatures lying there in cool
Sweet linen sheets, in slumber like the pool
Of moonlight white as water on the floor?
Will they come down laughing, and unlock the
    door?
And will they draw me in, and let me sit
On the tall settle while the lamp is lit?
And shall I see their innocent clean lives
Shining as plainly as the plates and knives,
The blue bowls, and the brass cage with its bird?

But listen! listen! Surely something stirred
Within the house, and creeping down the halls
Draws close to me with sinister footfalls.

Will long, pale fingers softly lift the latch,
And lead me up, under the osier thatch,
To a little room, a little secret room,
Hung with green arras picturing the doom,
The most disastrous death of some proud knight?
And shall I search the room by candle-light
And see, behind the curtains of my bed,
A murdered man who sleeps as sleep the dead?

Or will my clamorous knocking shake the trees
With lonely thunder through the stillnesses,
And then die down — the coldest fear of all —
To nothing, and deliberate silence fall
On the house deep in the silence, and no one come
To door or window, staring blind and dumb?

PHASES OF THE MOON

Once upon a time I heard
That the the flying moon was a Phoenix bird;
Thus she sails through windy skies,
Thus in the willow's arms she lies;
Turn to the East or turn to the West
In many trees she makes her nest.
When she's but a pearly thread
Look among birch leaves over-head;
When she dies in yellow smoke
Look in a thunder-smitten oak;
But in May when the moon is full,
Bright as water and white as wool,
Look for her where she loves to be,
Asleep in a high magnolia tree.

NADIR

If we must cheat ourselves with any dream,
Then let it be a dream of nobleness:
Since it is necessary to express
Gall from black grapes — to sew an endless seam
With a rusty needle — chase a spurious gleam
Narrowing to the nothing through the less —
Since life's no better than a bitter guess,
And love's a stranger — let us change the theme.

Let us at least pretend — it may be true —
That we can close our lips on poisonous
Dark wine diluted by the Stygean wave;
And let me dream sublimity in you,
And courage, liberal for the two of us:
Let us at least pretend we can be brave.

THE POOR OLD CANNON

Upbroke the sun
In red-gold foam;
Thus spoke the gun
At the Soldiers' Home:

" Whenever I hear
Blue thunder speak
My voice sounds clear
But little and weak.

" And when the proud
Young cockerels crow
My voice sounds loud,
But gentle and low.

" When the mocking-bird
Prolongs his note
I cannot be heard
Though I split my throat."

OCTOBER

Beauty has a tarnished dress,
And a patchwork cloak of cloth
Dipped deep in mournfulness,
Striped like a moth.

Wet grass where it trails
Dyes it green along the hem;
She has seven silver veils
With cracked bells on them.

She is tired of all these —
Gray gauze, translucent lawn;
The broad cloak of Herakles
Is tangled flame and fawn.

Water and light are wearing thin:
She has drawn above her head
The warm enormous lion skin
Rough gold and red.

OPHELIA

My locks are shorn for sorrow
   Of love which may not be;
Tomorrow and tomorrow
   Are plotting cruelty.

The winter wind tangles
   These ringlets half-grown,
The sun sprays with spangles
   And rays like his own.

Oh, quieter and colder
   Is the stream; he will wait;
When my curls touch my shoulder
   He will comb them straight.

POOR EARTH

It is not heaven: bitter seed
Leavens its entrails with despair:
It is a star where dragons breed:
Devils have a footing there.

The sky has bent it out of shape;
The sun has strapped it to his wheel;
Its course is crooked to escape
Traps and gins of stone and steel.

It balances on air, and spins
Snared by strong transparent space;
I forgive it all its sins;
I kiss the scars upon its face.

LOVE SONG

Lovers eminent in love
Ever diversities combine;
The vocal cords of the cushat-dove,
The snake's articulated spine.

Such elective elements
Educate the eye and lip
With one's refreshing innocence,
The other's claim to scholarship.

The serpent's knowledge of the world
Learn, and the dove's more naïve charm;
Whether your ringlets should be curled,
And why he likes his claret warm.

QUARREL

Let us quarrel for these reasons:
You detest the salt which seasons
My speech . . . and all my lights go out
In the cold poison of your doubt.
I love Shelley . . . you love Keats
Something parts and something meets.
I love salads . . . you love chops;
Something goes and something stops.
Something hides its face and cries;
Something shivers; something dies.
I love blue ribbons brought from fairs;
You love sitting splitting hairs.
I love truth, and so do you. . . .
Tell me, is it truly true?

DEATH AND THE MAIDEN

Fair youth with the rose at your lips,
A riddle is hid in your eyes;
Discard conversational quips,
Give over elaborate disguise.

The rose's funereal breath
Confirms my intuitive fears;
To prove your devotion, Sir Death,
Avaunt for a dozen of years.

But do not forget to array
Your terror in juvenile charms;
I shall deeply regret my delay
If I sleep in a skeleton's arms.

THE DOLL

*"For woman's manly god must not exceed
Proportions of the natural nursing size."*
GEORGE MEREDITH

I shaped him from almond paste
I gilded his nails,
I moulded him a wasp waist
In green swallow tails.

Under waxen eyelids
His eyes were black pearls;
His brows were thin as spider-threads
Traced in crescent curls.

I poured enamel, smooth as cream
To lacquer yellow locks;
I laid my creature of a dream
In a clear crystal box.

At midnight, at midnight,
I dance for his sake,
Suckling him on liquid light
And crumbs of honey-cake.

PRIMAVERA IN THE NORTH

She has danced for leagues and leagues,
Over thorns and thistles,
Prancing to a tune of Grieg's
Performed on willow whistles.

Antelopes behold her, dazed,
Velvet-eyed and furry;
Polar flowers, crackle-glazed,
Snap beneath her hurry.

In a wig of copper wire,
A gown of scalloped gauzes,
She capers like a flame of fire
Over Arctic mosses.

All her tears have turned to birds,
All her thoughts of dolour
Paint the snow with scarlet words
And traceries of colour.

THE IVORY STATUETTE

I'll leave you Phidias and Praxiteles,
Who out of marble made a prouder race
Scornful of man; I'll leave you Samothrace
And those broad wings, bright with the salt of
seas.
I'll have no arrogant gods as tall as trees,
But a small ivory statue, with a face
Minutely flawless, hair like golden lace;
Six inches, and all loveliness in these.

I'll have her carved by one who charmed those
flowers
We call Tanagras out of tinted clay;
Bronze shall she stand on, green as water is;
In a cool gallery of evening hours
Sequestered, to forget the squalid day,
And broken exiles from the Acropolis.

SALUTE

Riding down the avenue in the early morning
I passed a man who was going home to bed;
I was setting out and he was returning;
I was alive and he was dead.

I rode in a chariot of bright green metal
He in a chariot of dull black wood,
And each of us was too tired to settle
Whose luck was bad and whose luck good.

The street flowed molten — a white-hot level;
Smoothly we passed in our painted hells;
I bowed my head to the other poor devil;
His was bowed before Someone Else.

I the waker and he the sleeper
Passed where the pearly dust hung thick;
He rode down where the dust lay deeper;
My dime went into the slot with a click.

LOVE TO STEPHEN

Cherub in armor;
Wolf in rabbit-skin;
New wine, far more
Harsh than its habit-skin;
Nice rice pudding;
Bonaparte brandy;
Hellebore brooding
On peppermint candy.
Apple-cheeked shepherd-boy
Giants make irate;
Gunpowder-peppered boy;
Mild-mannered pirate,
Strung from the yard-arm
For flying a skull-and-bones;
Strong in the sword-arm
To punish the sullen bones
Of Mitching Malecho
Or defend Queen Guinevere.
Red and white calico
Banded with miniver;
Sometimes a stag you are,
Sometimes a stallion,
Sometimes a jaguar
Or a Spanish galleon
Raiding the Azores;

Beneath a silk mitten
Your fingers are razors.
A wild-cat kitten
Striped black and furry tan,
Trussed in a uniform
Tight and Puritan.
Queer as cuneiform;
A scarlet rocket
And a clean tin dipper;
David Crockett
And a Salem skipper.
A canvas of Rembrandt's
Might seem your proper field —
But — the resemblance
To Master Copperfield!
Perhaps, in small ways,
A starched child-chorister,
But fierce, and always
Robin Hood's forester.
Who shall draw
Or tell your story
Brother, in-law
And in outlawry?

THE HEART UPON THE SLEEVE

Dear Heart, behold you bound
Upon a ragged sleeve,
And no one will believe
The emblem of the wound.

Good Heart, because I wear
Your colour on my arm,
A shield, a trefoil charm,
That turns a sword in air,

They take you for a patch
Upon the tattered cloth;
A mournful lunar moth,
A bird they cannot catch;

A tinsel favour tied
Above the living vein;
They take you for a stain
Of vanity and pride.

Poor Heart, and are you pierced,
Though frivolously worn
The arrow, and the thorn
Where bleeds a rose reversed?

Remember it is well
That no one can perceive
These drops upon my sleeve,
Which are invisible.

Never the carrion beak
Shall taste transparent blood
Whose pulse in solitude
Adores and does not break.

Be well content, dear Heart,
To wear a light disguise
For fear a vulture flies
To tear your strings apart.

RESTORATION LOVE SONG

I love you more than life:
  How small a thing to say
When Atropos her knife
  Can never cut away
A stronger thread than clay
  Plaited of fear and grief!
Therefore, my lord, be gay;
  I love you more than life.

I love you more than death:
  How solemn a thing to swear!
When this dissolving breath
  Is heaviest to bear,
What blessed relief it were
  To loose the bonds of faith!
Therefore, my lord, beware;
  I love you more than death.

I love you more than these:
  Such doors are shut and slammed;
Somewhere beyond is peace,
  And sweets compact and crammed;
And bread is buttered and jammed;
  And wine has honey lees;
Therefore, my lord, be damned,
  If I love you more than these!

ODE AGAINST PUBLIC SPIRIT

Call all the stars from Mars to Sagittarius
And mould them to a mirrored pyramid;
Invoke the rivers blue and green and various
As languid snakes who ripple as they're bid;
Make the high hills troop forth in loving-kind-
    ness;
Summon the sun, and strike the sky to blind-
    ness;
And fill the lagoon
With the moon's pure essence,
Though dark of the moon
And lacking her presence;
Now let her lustre be no longer hid.

This punishment the beautiful has merited;
It must be disciplined and made to work
In ways impersonal and public-spirited;
The Southern Cross, conversion of the Turk;
The silver crescent, any foreign mission
For introducing peace or prohibition;
And the rose-coloured birds
And the bronze-coloured foxes
Must memorize words
About ballot-boxes,
And eloquence from Cicero to Burke.

But leave me, somewhere in the fading dahlias,
A rainbow midge, no bigger than the eye
Of one minutest singing-bird of Thalia's,
Who, in obscurity, elects to cry,
Under a violet canopy of quiet,
Like young Catullus or Sir Thomas Wyatt,
Bright as a prism,
Strong as a giant,
Shouting a schism
Loud and defiant.
In holy rage, to break his heart and die.

LITTLE JOKE

Stripping an almond tree in flower
    The wise apothecary's skill
A single drop of lethal power
    From perfect sweetness can distil.

From bitterness in efflorescence,
    With murderous poisons packed therein;
The poet draws pellucid essence
    Pure as a drop of metheglin.

VENETIAN INTERIOR

Allegra, rising from her canopied dreams,
Slides both white feet across the slanted beams
Which lace the peacock jalousies: behold
An idol of fine clay, with feet of gold.

HIGH WIND

Boeotius laughed upon the windy corner's
Incline; my female ancestors were shocked,
Investing eyes like mid-Victorian mourners'
With veils of fear; but one among them mocked.

She only, careless and aristocratic,
Laughed with Boeotius, laughing in his face,
And stared, in disarray divinely static,
While slave-ships foundered under Samothrace.

THE PEKINGESE

FOR A PICTURE

This Pekingese, that makes the sand-grains spin,
Is digging little tunnels to Pekin:
Dream him emerging in a porcelain cave
Where wounded dragons stain a pearly wave.

CURIOUS CIRCUMSTANCE

The sailorman's child
And the girl of the witch —
They can't be defiled
By touching pitch.

The sailorman's son
Had a ship for his nursery;
The other one
Was baptized by sorcery.

Although he's shipped
To the Persian Gulf, her
Body's been dipped
In burning sulphur.

NOTES

I

Beltane. Deciphered by Jane D. Wise. Late. Beltane is the Celtic name for the First of May, celebrated with two fires by the Druids. E. W. had probably in her mind the idea of Druidical sacrifice.

"Since We Can Neither Run Nor Hide." Deciphered by Jane D. Wise. Probably late. The idea of flight and escape persisted through E. W.'s poetry because of the circumstances of her earlier life. It engendered always an attitude of courage, either defiant or stoic.

"I Saw Milton Stand Alone." Deciphered by Jane D. Wise. Late. Obviously the beginning of a poem that might have developed a discussion of the Church of Christ as affecting the attitude of two great poets. The influence of Shelley in Elinor's life is referred to by Miss Olivier. E. W. was also a great admirer of the grandeur of Milton's verse.

Green Apple. Deciphered by Jane D. Wise. The first line repeats the last line of Blake's famous lyric on Milton. Blake's poetry was well-loved by E. W. She was fond of quoting the last verse from "The Land of Dreams." The poem is of a personal emotional experience.

Firth of Forth. Deciphered by Jane D. Wise. Late. One of E. W.'s unfinished ballads, yet so full of characteristic striking phrase and vivid pictorial quality as to assert its right to inclusion. E. W. was thoroughly familiar with Percy's "Reliques" and other ballad literature and particularly admired the Scotch contribution to balladry.

Three Elegies. Deciphered by Jane D. Wise. Late. The ironic ending of this poem only underlines E. W.'s passion for poetry. Interesting in this connection, as referring to their frequent argument as to the respective merits of Keats and Shelley, is the fourth of the poems beginning Part Three of Edna St. Vincent Millay's "Huntsman, What Quarry?" a group of five poems addressed to E. W. It is the second of two sonnets, the first one reappearing in Miss Millay's "Collected Sonnets" and titled "To Elinor Wylie." See also the poem in this volume, "A Skylark at Steepletop."

Subversive Sonnets. Deciphered by Jane D. Wise. Late. See remarks in "Foreword."

Sonnet — "Courage and lovingkindness are approved." Deciphered by Jane D. Wise. Compare sonnet on page 308 of "Collected Poems."

Sonnet — "Is he not fortunate that he is freed." Deciphered by Jane D. Wise. Late. See Editorial Note to Miss Olivier's "Concerning Elinor Wylie."

The Thread has been transcribed by Jane D. Wise from a pencilled ms., on blue paper, of indeterminate date. The title has been furnished by the Editor. In the original, the fourth word in the third line of the second verse might either be "tinseled" or "threaded," but the former word has been chosen as more probable.

II

The Golden Heifer. Deciphered by Jane D. Wise. See reference to this poem in " Foreword."

III

Roses in Winter. Written in Washington, D. C., January 1920. First unprinted poem of E. W.'s (aside from poems in " Incidental Numbers ") seen by W. R. B.

City Morning. Deciphered from holograph ms. by W. R. B.

Spring. In ms. typed. Probably early.

From the Wall. In ms. typed. Circa 1922. Title suggested to E. W. by Leonora Speyer.

At The Hospital. In ms. both holograph and typed. Early. *Chose vue.*

With a Blue Honey-Jar Full of Flowers. In ms. typed. Probably later.

A Skylark at Steepletop. In ms. typed. " Steepletop " is the home of Edna St. Vincent Millay, at Austerlitz, N. Y. See note to *Three Elegies.*

Far Away. Deciphered from holograph ms. by W. R. B. Late.

Silver Bells and Cockle Shells. In ms. typed. Probably late.

Witches. In ms. typed. Probably early.

" *— In a Country Churchyard.*" In ms. typed. Circa 1921.

" *Advice to the Lovelorn.*" In ms. typed. Referred to in " Foreword " to " Collected Poems."

Chinese Priest. In ms. typed. Early.

Sonnet — "*Whether you grind your teeth in giving it.*" In ms. typed. Late.

Sonnet — "*When in the dear beginning of the fever.*" In ms. typed. Late. Quite possibly a sonnet rejected from the sequence "One Person" in "Angels and Earthly Creatures."

A Lodging for the Night. In ms. typed. Late.

The Pillars of the Temple. In ms. typed. Late.

IV

"*Les Lauriers Sont Coupés.*" See Foreword. In "Incidental Numbers," dated May 1911, the poet then being in her twenty-fourth year. Reprinted in *Contemporary Verse* May 1920, and in "The Contemporary Verse Anthology," E. P. Dutton & Co. 1920. "Incidental Numbers" was printed in 1912 by William Clowes & Sons Ltd., London, England.

Written on the Flyleaf of John Webster's Plays. See "Foreword." This sonnet is contemporaneous with "The Knight Fallen on Evil Days" which in "Incidental Numbers" bears the date of May 1911. Even if later it is sufficiently remarkable. It was first printed in *The Phoenix Nest* of *The Saturday Review of Literature,* April 9, 1927.

South of The Potomac. First printed in Christopher Morley's column, *The Bowling Green, New York Evening Post,* July 1, 1920. Reprinted in "The Bowling Green: An Anthology of Verse." Selected by Christopher Morley. Doubleday, Page & Company. 1924. Written in Washington, D. C.

The Child on the Curbstone. Ditto as above. First printed September 28, 1920.

The Lost Path. Century Magazine. November 1920.

Phases of the Moon. Contemporary Verse. Circa 1921. Year Book of Poetry Society of South Carolina. 1922.

Nadir. Published in this form in a brochure issued by Mahlon Leonard Fisher, having been submitted to his magazine, *The Sonnet* (afterward discontinued), August 16, 1921, by Bernice Lesbia Kenyon with whom E. W. then shared an apartment in New York City. She wrote Mr. Fisher " My friend, Mrs. Wylie, would like . . . to have you look at her latest sonnet, and discover whether you can use it." The above information is from Mr. Fisher's brochure copyright by him 1937 at Williamsport in Pennsylvania. One hundred copies of the folder were printed in the month of June 1937. It bears the title " The First Printing of a Wylie Sonnet." Mr. Fisher is in error there, as " Les Lauriers Sont Coupés " appeared earlier and the sonnet " Atavism " in a group called " Still Colors " appeared in *Poetry: A Magazine of Verse* in April 1921, having been accepted by Harriet Monroe, January 20, 1920. In the original version " Nadir " was called " Casual Sonnet," and a change was made in line 5, the original line reading, " With a rusty needle — to pursue a gleam, etc." To be mentioned along with Mr. Fisher's folder is another folder of a poem by E. W. presented to the New York Public Library by Harvey Taylor, May 8, 1935. The text is " Rondeau. (*A Windy Day.*) " which originally appeared in " Incidental Numbers," dated " Summer of 1904." 100 copies of this folder were issued, of which the Rare Book Room of the Library has No. 69. A note (*verso* of the folder) says " Earliest known poem by Elinor Wylie " and states that in stanza two, in the first line, the word " will " has been changed to " must " " by Nancy Hoyt, sister of the poet." The line is so changed, but the first poem from " Incidental Numbers " used in Nancy Hoyt's " Elinor Wylie: The Portrait of an Unknown Lady " is the " Paolo and Francesca " sonnet, dated " Summer of 1902," which is actually the earliest poem of Elinor's ever to be printed. Incidentally, though among her " Juvenilia," as is the " Rondeau," this is her earliest sonnet to be printed. The rhyme scheme is, Shakespearian, a,b,a,b,c,d,c,d,e,f,e,f,g,g. It was written at the age of fifteen.

The Poor Old Cannon. First printed by Christopher Mor ley in his column and anthology as above mentioned; original appearance June 6, 1921.

October. Ditto. Date of October 13, 1921.

Ophelia. Smart Set, October 1921. Reprinted in " The Smart Set Anthology." Reynal & Hitchcock, Inc. 1934.

Poor Earth. The Literary Review of *The New York Evening Post.* Feb. 18, 1922.

Love Song. Vanity Fair. August 1922.

Quarrel. Century Magazine. December 1922.

Death and The Maiden. Vanity Fair, March 1923. The accompanying drawing by Charles Martin. On page 51. On page 54 of the same issue appeared E. W.'s now famous poem, " A Strange Story." At this time E. W. was poetry editor of *Vanity Fair.*

The Doll. Vanity Fair. April 1923. This was accompanied by a drawing by Rockwell Kent. In the same issue, on page 63, appeared a portrait of E. W. by Nikolas Muray with (in part) the following caption: " Mrs. Wylie's poetry gives the effect of bright metals and jewels melted by a single intense flame and poured molten into rigorous moulds which, when the fluid has cooled, stamp it with the hard mark of permanence." Under this appeared two poems, titled " Portraits in The Sonnet Form " I–II. The first is the sonnet called " Unfinished Portrait " which appeared originally in " Black Armour " and stands on page 86 of the " Collected Poems." In the magazine it began differently, " Mercutio, my hand has never used —." The second was reprinted in " Black Armour " under the title of " King Honour's Eldest Son " and stands upon page 71 of the " Collected Poems." In the following issue of *Vanity Fair,* May 1923, appeared as a " Literary Hors d'Oeuvre " the poet's prose piece, " The Two Glass Doors," never collected. In June of that year her " Dramatic Dialogue in the Manner of Molnar and Other Hungarians " was signed Mollie MacMichael, and thereafter the name " Mollie MacMichael " or the initials, " M.M.", on the advertising page called " In Vanity Fair," indicated work by Elinor Wylie. In January and February 1924 her contributions to this literary sort of advertisement of the magazine were " My Sphinx, Yvonne " and " The Eternal Triangle."

Primavera in the North. Vanity Fair. July 1923. Drawing by Rockwell Kent. E. W.'s pseudonym " Mollie Mac-Michael."

Salute. The Saturday Review of Literature. March 21, 1925. *Chose vue.*

Love to Stephen. The Bookman. June 1927. To Stephen Vincent Benét.

The Heart Upon the Sleeve. Poetry: A Magazine of Verse. May 1928.

Restoration Love Song. The New Yorker. March 30, 1929.

Ode Against Public Spirit. Posthumously printed by Christopher Morley in *The Bowling Green* of *The Saturday Review of Literature.* April 24, 1937.

Little Joke. First printed in Christopher Morley's column, *The Bowling Green, New York Evening Post,* January 12, 1921. Reprinted in "The Bowling Green" anthology as described above.

Venetian Interior. New Republic. July 27, 1921.

High Wind. First printed by Christopher Morley as above, April 18, 1922.

The Pekingese. Century Magazine. April 1922.

Curious Circumstance. First printed by Christopher Morley 1922. Not in "The Bowling Green" anthology.

INDEX OF FIRST LINES